Evincepub
Publishing

i

# Evincepub Publishing

Nehru Nagar, Bilaspur, Chhattisgarh 495001
First Published by Evincepub Publishing 2021
Copyright © CHIRAG SHARMA 2021
All Rights Reserved.
**ISBN:** 978-93-5446-235-1

# UNREVEALED
## SOFT AND DANGEROUS POETRY

CHIRAG SHARMA

# ABOUT THE BOOK

Learning lessons of life at an early age was not what I had decided. In fact it was the decision of destiny that made me write my heart out today. In a smooth going life we find things and people bracing but when tragedy turns your track you realize the importance of people and relations you are tagged to.

Unrevealed, soft and dangerous poetry is the output of the same that teaches a person the importance of beings and relations that work wonders. Bitter truth is the base I choose to design my dream, that's today in front of you. I don't want any of you to face similar situations which break you completely and later you repent their return for missing things. Live your life to the fullest but do not forget to tell people how each one of them holds a precious place in your heart.

In this mean world

God gifted you a universe

Which consists of some lovely people,
family and friends to face the worse.

In these exhausting times we realized import of people, some friends passed boundaries irrespective of virus fear and some sons carried their mothers alone to the cremation ground which impelled me to write my thoughts out.

# ABOUT THE AUTHOR

Born on 27th February 2001 in Shimla, Himachal Pradesh normal boy believer of the saying science is my passion and literature is love this is my first work that is being published and wish to come up with many more. In school days being an active participant in number of school plays, narrations to design and cast small dance dramas where I learnt a number of things, awarded for different cultural activities to officially attending theater workshops. Completed intermediate from Dayanand Public School Shimla and presently pursuing B.Sc life sciences second year of graduation from COE Sanjauli and working as a social worker in a renowned Rotaract club in Shimla as Director of Vocational Services.

All India winner of elocution competition organized by CSIR National Institution of science technology and development studies and VIBHA INDIA

We belong to land of mountains we believe in
simple living and sound relations and same we wish
to see in people .

# SPECIAL THANKS

Special thanks to all the lovely people around me. Heartfelt gratitude to my parents (Smt Shish Kala Sharma) and (Lt. Shri Balbir Sharma) for everything you people have done for me and my elder sister (Shagun) for being a constant support and a helping hand. Paying honour to feets of my Guru (Ms. Meena Sharma) for being the guiding light in this entire journey. A major thanks to all the teachers and friends for moulding me into the person I am today.

Chirag Sharma

# TABLE OF CONTENTS

# MESSAGE TO HEAVEN

I stay to say in the evening

Papa what's in your pocket for my childhood

cravings

With a smile he would say

 There's nothing today

For the things he has done for me

 I realized later when he set me free

 For the lessons and morals he had taught

Now life examines me with dreadful thoughts

The thank you I failed to say

Remained with me for your pray

On the death bed when you laid

 My hands folded for your heavens aid

Still waiting for my phone to ring with name 'DAD'

 Your absence has often made me sad

Deep inside my heart I drop tears

 Because I still have those old fears

It was you, your hands, your love and the precious

hug

Your son waits for you to hold your empty mug

A new home called heaven you have now

To see your son's wow.

# NEXT DAY

Be prepared for the next day

The day you don't know

Whether happiness or hardest in flow

Yes the day you don't know

Fears come and go through

Losing them or precious you

Whether wonder working day to do

Or it may make you low

Yes the day you don't know

Day brings sunshine

But don't forget some days are not fine

Day may bring things to you

 Or may take the best to grow

Yes the day you don't know

If we think of the next day

Forgetting the past way

Learning lessons from what we did

Refreshing ourselves with fresh blow

Yes the day you don't know

One who knows that a day will come

Of all the lessons you have already done

You will win the day

With a different glow

Yes the day you don't know

# SEPARATION SIN

I waited for the things to be fine

For you to come back and shine

Not sharing things became common

And you not wearing my gifted cotton

Promises which made us together

Was a lying ladder

For what has drifted us apart

Was never a hope to support smart

Ego and that respective pinch

Laid between us since

If we could have worked upon

We might have stayed in same lawn

Separating souls was our own decision

Hence we failed in great parent vision

Dividing riches was a clitch of law

Our child's broken heart we never saw

A prayer I make today

Of not dividing days and ways

Parents should never win

The separation sin

They must stay together forever and ever

And no small heart says

My parents don't stay together.

# GURU

In this stroll of life

We come across a number of teachers

But one who catches your heart

 Provides you the Secret path

Helps you work on your weakness

A special connection with uniqueness

It's difficult to find this master

Saving you from the disaster

Is then called guru

Lifelong you'll remember

Because now he's your family member

Often worshipped in prayers

Supporting you in your dares

Guru is hard to find

He knows what goes in mind

It's not so simple to be blessed with a guru

But if one is he is certainly true

Writing these lines I pay honour to his Lotus feet

Oh guru ji please help me succeed

# **LESSON**

Some lessons are learnt

Some are taught

Some by others

Some by mothers

Lessons from school

Lessons for fools

Lessons for need

Lessons that feed

Life is all about learning lessons

To assist rational reasons

A good learner lends help

To prove vigor of lessons to self

Some lessons I have learnt

Today those I confront

Tears only make your heart feel light

But what helps is your social life

Sharing hands today with someone

Will help you one day when you are undone

Relations don't stand by give and take

Here works your loves faith

You will always think when will these lessons pay off
Yes the day you see off

# WE WAIT FOR YOU TO FLY

The day she will fly

All the sinner men will die

Place where she will step

The success would feel shy

When she will retrieve her inner self

Mirror would reflect a bossy shine

Shine that shuts all the expectations of the worst

She will see the evil spirits shudder and cry

Her name will echo all around

Her importance would be measured in pound

But the actual anomaly appears

When she will realize the day she will fly

# TIPS OF SUCCESS

If you wish to succeed

You need to mend your deed

Thinking reading these tips will help

You are mistaken to your inner self

Efforts for success are distinct

Finding them with others is not the strength

Unaccompanied you need to combine

In a way to rise and shine

You might get inaccurate at a step or two

And only your heart knows you are true

It may skip a turn

Stay positive it will return

It's not effortless

To hold the Cup in a gentle fest

Never forget to respect and request

Never think you are done

For success always run

The day you overpower

The eminent success star

You will come to know

Tips of success were within you

 since far and far

For this happy hour

# UNIQUENESS

The worthy trait that lies within you

Unadorned to take but is elegant in view

Yes the same thing you might feel ashamed of

Is the real key for your take off

Take off to the world

Which can never understand and feel

But is off sensational value in an antiquated being

For he has seen life to the closest

Anne knows uniqueness is best

When nothing stands by your side

The same unadorned trait works bright

The precious gift your mother gifted you

Materialistic things may come and go

But it remains embedded within you

Things which make you distinct from others

Gifting each one of us the unique feathers

# SOUNDS OF SOCIETY

I can't understand the society we live in
Here crowds are gathered for useless things
But when we require they think it's nothing
No one has the part to stand alone
And if one does he's definitely gone
Boys tagged with toy cars
Shameful to see a girl with scars
Here beauty has a different definition
For them heart is a useless creation
I can't understand the society we live in
We divided humanity into caste
Even God failed in being so fast
Restrictions for them we made
Poor fellows their innocence always paid
Our society comes with precious notions
Boys don't cry as if they don't have emotions
I can't understand this society we live in
Here connectors are described on your respective
act
Excuse me who the hell are you to decide that

It hardly bothers what a person face

It's all destroyed from a certain base

Oh God they should never win

I can't understand the society we live in

Well mistakes of past cannot be revised

Drop all the old notions and think a little wise

The great change always lies in you

Start your rules and stop being fools

Then we could amend the old fin

But still I can't understand the society we living.

# CIRCUMSTANCE

Don't worry if you get stuck in a circumstance

Life always gives you another chance

Forehand of Clock always comes from 6 to 8

Don't let situations destroy your faith

Scenes often split our souls

Don't worry friend we need to control

Every dying tree has the power to grow once again

Always remember these circumstances are created and gained

We cried today blaming God

Often questioning what have I done Lord

Not realizing how we misused things

That has today resulted in cutting our wings

Working hard now to come out and fly

But what about that silent cry

Result of your sin

Do you think now you could win

Finally if you wish to come out of a situation

Mend your mistakes with innovation

Never spoil your past

Always stay gentle and kind

Be aware of the next circumstance you find

# WAS IT OR NOT

There is only one thing I want to ask you

If someday my soul meets yours

Was it easy to leave?

Was it or not

Easy to leave the ones you loved without a doubt

The ones you couldn't stay a day without

Just tell me once

Was it or not

Easy to just leave our hand and vanish

Those memories haunt us the ones we used to

cherish

When your soul meets mine

 In the heaven that's so divine

One thing just one thing to ask

Was it or not

Easy to leave us with a smiling mask

There are so many things to ask

Please come back with the whole life

Because these tears are not easy to wipe

# A PERFECT FRIEND

The one who's  there by your side

No matter time and situations you hide

He might not say

But you are his family right

He gets hurt for the things people laugh

And there lies the reason he would win your heart

You feel free to say your if and but

And he will never say shut up

He is a perfect guide to you

For he loves you the way you do

I feel happy for him making place in my parents
heart

But wait what if they throw me apart

He holds a great hug

That you need in bad times

We love to share those naughty rhymes

Reality check the perfect being is to you

Or you catching the love flu

Here never stands the bar of age

He knows you will never change

Drift and turn

Is what life brings in return

No matter right or wrong

The one to sing you birthday song

If you truly love the bond that exists

Never try to shift

# BROKEN MOTHER

For that mother who always thought

She will go to heaven's abode on shoulders of her

son

Thinking it would be great fun

But that thought today tangled

Phone call that ended things

Late night now people entered with her son

She's  still waiting for him to say

come down Ma to pick these tons

A loud cry she gave

Get up get up you better behave

Someone hugged her and said

Grandma is my dad dead

She wanted her soul to leave and be sure

She reaches there before

Her heart was not ready to say that goodbye

To the son who always talked about Sky

She thought to end her life

But there she saw her son's wife

Who was still not in sense

Because she failed in defense

Cries all around

Their being they didn't find

Sunrise was there the next day

How to wake him up there's no way

Difficult to feel what you've lost

Poor mother paid a precious cost